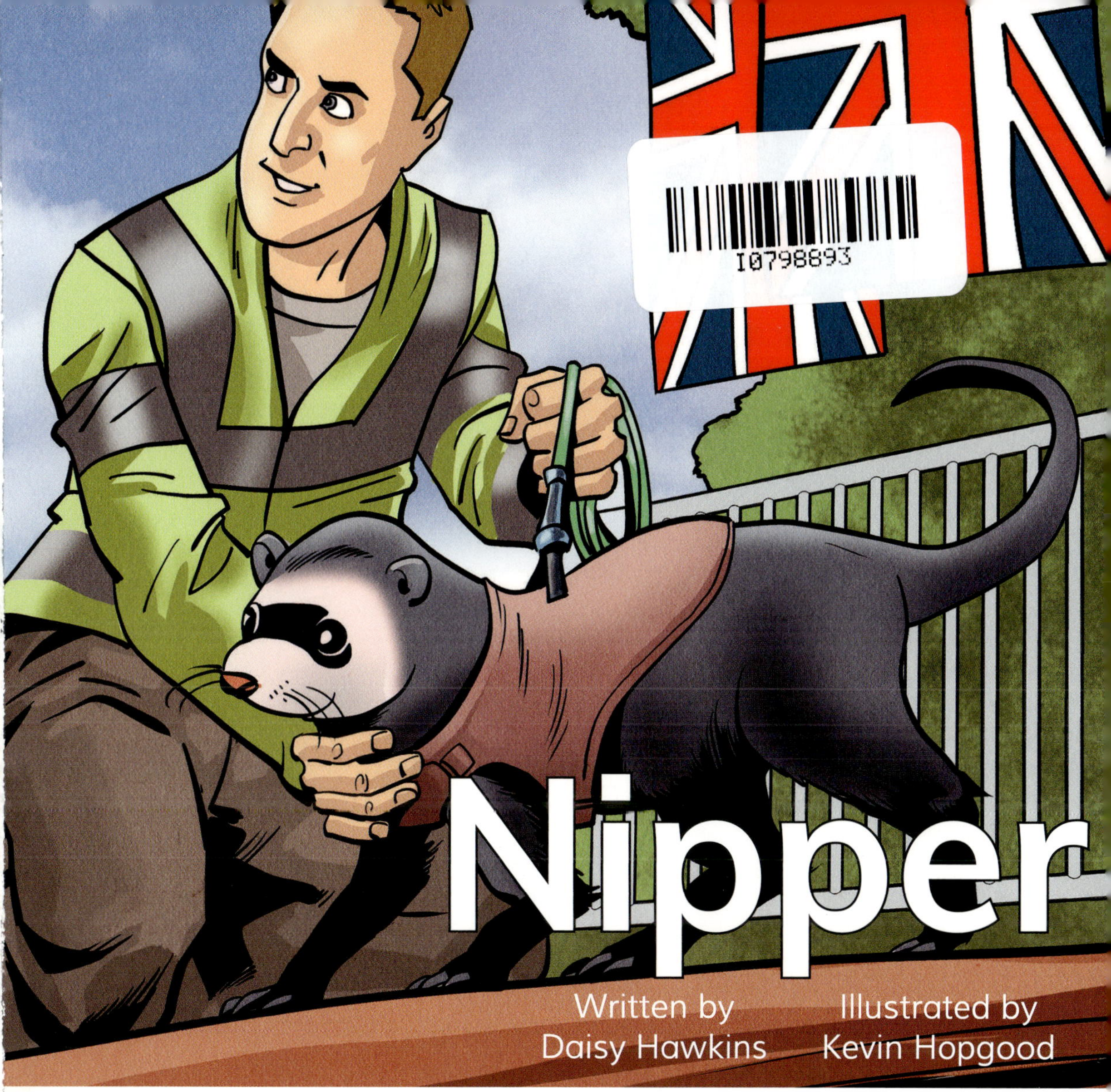

Nipper

Written by
Daisy Hawkins

Illustrated by
Kevin Hopgood

ıblished in 2026 by
orwood House Press
544 Clinton Street
ıffalo, NY 14224

ɪnted in the United States of America

Library of Congress Cataloging-in-Publication Data:
Names: Hawkins, Daisy, author. | Hopwood, Kevin, illustrator.
Title: Nipper / written by Daisy Hawkins, illustrated by Kevin Hopgood.
Ferrets as pets / written by Daisy Hawkins.
Description: Buffalo, NY : Norwood House Press, 2026. | Series: Phonics all-stars: phase 3 |
Identifiers: ISBN 9781978578029 (pbk.) | ISBN 9781978578036 (library bound) | ISBN 9781978578043 (ebook)
Subjects: LCSH: Reading–Phonetic method–Juvenile literature. | English language–Phonetics–Juvenile literature. | Ferret–Juvenile literature. | Ferrets as pets–Juvenile literature.
Classification: LCC LB1573.3 H395 2026 | DDC 372.465–dc23

CPSIA compliance information: Batch #CW26NHP: For further information contact Norwood House Press at 1-800-237-9932.

Back in 1981 ...
We need this wedding on TV for all to see.

Yes, but the TV cord needs to go under the road. And to go under the road, the TV cord has to go in that tunnel.
That is not a tunnel!
This is not good.

Wait! An animal might fit! Nipper might fit!

In a garden not far-off ...
I need you, Nipper. We all need you.

Back at the tunnel ...
This is madness. Pure madness.
Um, is that rat up to the job?

Nipper is a ferret, Ben, not a rat. And she **is** up to it.
Let me get her secure in her harness. Then we can add the TV cord.

The cord is light and food will lure her down the tunnel. It will be quick if we meet her with this.
OK, I am in. I will man this bit. You go and meet her with the food.
Shall I inform the queen that a ferret is on the job?

Let her go!
Go on, Nipper! For king and queen!

You did it, Nipper. Now all of us can see the big wedding.
All hail to the rat!

Nipper the ferret, 1981

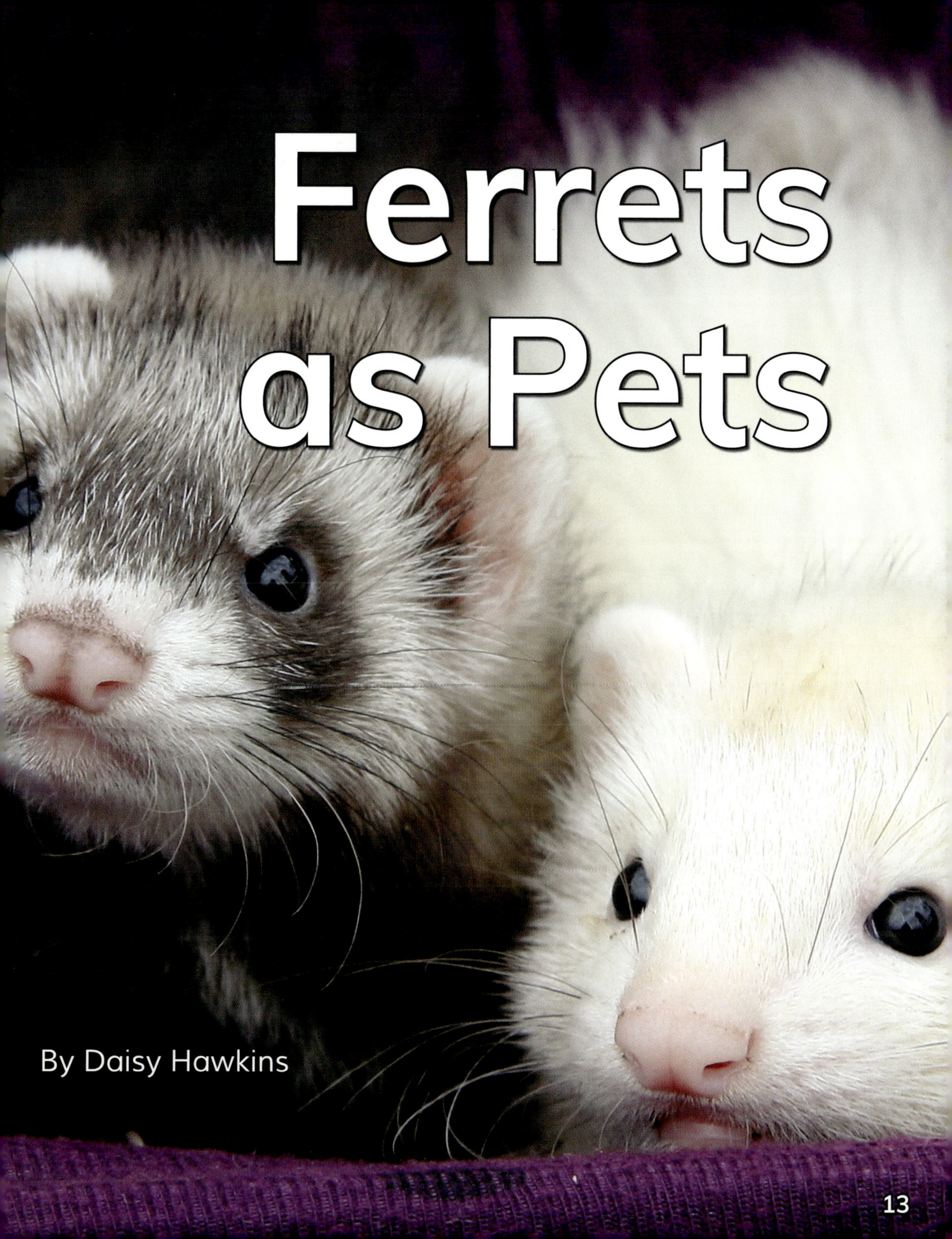

Ferrets as Pets

By Daisy Hawkins

This is a ferret.

Ferrets can be good pets.

You can get ferrets with dark coats ...

... and ferrets with light coats.

Pet ferrets all need shelter and a bed.

They need room to run – and food too.

Not this sort of food ...

... but this sort of food.

Food such as rats, chicken wings, and bits of rabbit or beef.

You can pick ferrets up.

Her ferret seems good with this, but not all ferrets are.

If they are not, you can get a ferret harness.

If it is hot, you need to keep ferrets cool. Hot sunlight and thick fur is not a good mix.

Her ferret keeps cool in a pool.

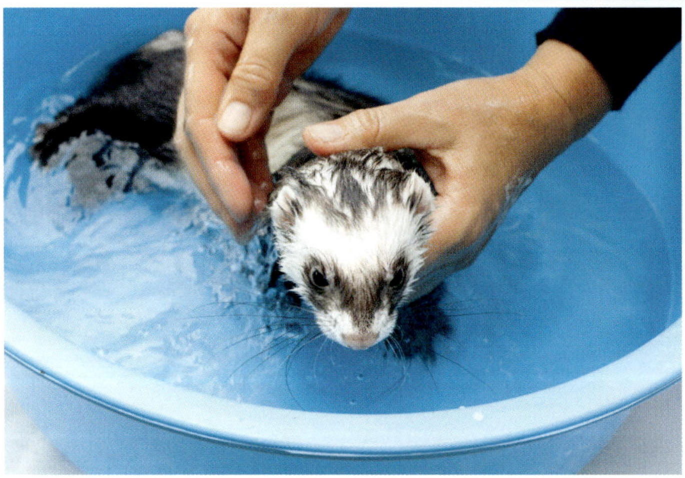

Visit a vet if a ferret is unwell or in pain. Vets can get ear wax and cut long nails too.

As ferrets are smart, you can get them to go in a litter box.

Will you get a pet ferret?